Legendary Business

From Rats to Riche$ Workbook

Sharon Galluzzo

Copyright © 2016 Sharon Galluzzo

All rights reserved. No part of this book may be reproduced, stored, or transmitted by any means whether auditory, graphic, mechanical, or electronic without written permission of both publisher and author, except in the case of brief excerpts used in critical articles and reviews. Unauthorized reproduction of any part of this work is illegal and is punishable by law.

ISBN-10: 1-944662-08-1

ISBN-13: 978-1-944662-08-0

RP

REALIZATION PRESS

Realization Press Publishing date: 11/08/2016

Cover Design by Nathaniel Dasco

Contents

Chapter 1 The Pied Piper 1

Chapter 2 Maya Ratt 4

Chapter 3 Holden Ratt 7

Chapter 4 Darnell Ratt 10

Chapter 5 Charles Ratt 14

Chapter 6 Charlotte Ratt 17

Chapter 7 ACTION TEAM 21

Chapter 8 Now It's Your Turn 22

What's Next? 23

Introduction

Welcome to *Legendary Business: From Rats to Riche$ Workbook*. It is designed to be a companion piece to the book by the same name. If you don't yet have a copy of the book, you can find it here: www.LegendaryBusiness.net.

Getting the rats out of your business takes some doing and the "work" in this workbook is just that. Take your time. Put thought into your answers. Slacking off will only hurt your business and allow the rats free reign in your business.

You know your business should move forward. You know there is MORE and you want it. Don't wait.

Nothing changes until you move, so let's get going!!

Chapter 1

Pages 1-6 in *Legendary Business: From Rats to Riche$*

The Pied Piper

Your business is infested with rats. Not actual living and breathing rodents, but figurative vermin that keep you from reaching the success you want and causing your business to be sick. *Legendary Business: From Rats to Riche$* helps you identify some of the rats in your business and ways to get rid of them. But no mystical flute player is on his way – you have to be your OWN Pied Piper. Find your sheet music here.

1. In a couple of sentences, explain your business.

2. Who do you serve?

3. Describe your customers. (Age, interests, gender, location, etc.)

4. How do you connect with your customers?

5. How do you feel about your customers?

6. How do your customers feel about you/your business?

7. What do you like most in your business?

8. What do you like least in your business?

9. What is your definition of success?

10. List the top 3 challenges you currently have in your business.

      A.

      B.

      C.

11. What do you see as the causes of the business challenges listed above?

      A.

      B.

      C.

Are the following statements True or False for you and your business? Be honest. No one is grading your test.

12. You know what you do, but your market does not.

    True or False

13. You are constantly busy but your business is not moving forward.

    True or False

14. You struggle with the parts of your business that you do not like to do.

    True or False

15. You are attracted to all the new and exciting "things" for businesses like social media, training courses, books, etc but find you often do not follow through to completion.

    True or False

16. You know you want to be successful but you can't figure out what is missing.

    True or False

17. You are working hard day in and day out but still not getting where you want to go.

    True or False

If you answered true to at least one of these statements, then *Legendary Business: From Rats to Riche$* is for you! You are in the right place to become the Pied Piper and make your business legendary.

Chapter 2

Pages 9-18 in *Legendary Business: From Rats to Riche$*

Maya Ratt

Maya only wants to do the "fun stuff" in her business. She neglects her business and shuns the money-making tasks because they don't fulfill her.

1. How do the traits of Maya Ratt manifest themselves in your business? How are you like Maya?

2. List areas where Maya is stealing your sustenance and making your business more difficult.

3. List the five top-selling items or services in your business last year. Use the raw numbers of actual sales.

    A.

    B.

    C.

    D.

    E.

4. Of these items, which is the most profitable? (How much money you get to keep after costs.)

5. Rank the top five items above in order from most profitable to least.

    Most

    A.

    B.

    C.

    D.

    E.

    Least

6. Were the results of surprising to you? Why or why not?

7. How can you refocus (if necessary) your marketing and advertising to get more sales for the most profitable items?

8. What needs to change in your business so Maya is out the door and you are making more money?

9. List necessary/required tasks in your business that drain your energy.

10. What motivates you?

11. What is your best motivational technique for getting difficult tasks done?

12. Create a fun motivation for yourself right now! Brainstorm. When you accomplish X you get to Y (or something like that). Make this a total WIN for you. Alternatively, if you are negatively motivated, list the "hurt" that happens if you don't achieve a task.

13. List five motivations can you use every day in your business. Make sure you put one of these into motion the next time you need it!

    HOT TIP: Write or print this list and post it where you can see it every day while you work.

    A.

    B.

    C.

    D.

    E.

14. Remember, nothing changes until you move. You must be in ACTION! From this chapter choose ONE THING that you will implement right away in your business. There may be several, but choose the one that excites you and makes the biggest impact on your business.

15. Now go back and add dates for completion of your ONE THING. Put it on your calendar right now!

Would you like more support? The PLAN Piper Village on Facebook is for you. Join the private group just to get advice, tips, answers to trick questions and lots more! We are here to help you through your journey, you don't have to go it alone!
Ask to join here: https://www.facebook.com/groups/ThePLANPiper/

Chapter 3

Pages 21-30 in *Legendary Business: From Rats to Riche$*

Holden Ratt

Holden has no plan, no direction, no goals. He works all month to pay the bills, never knowing if he will have enough, fall short or make a profit.

1. How do the traits of Holden Ratt manifest themselves in your business? How are you like Holden?

2. List areas where Holden is stealing your sustenance and making your business more difficult.

3. Do you have written goals for all areas of your business? If not, start here to begin setting goals. If you already have goals, answer these questions to see if you are still on track.

4. What do you want from and for your business?

5. How do you define "success"?

6. How much money do you need to pay the bills?

7. How much more money/profit do you want to make beyond paying the bills?

8. How much to do you want to sell each month and year (sales goals)?

9. How much money do you want to save?

10. How much do you want/need to improve productivity or increase inventory?

11. How quickly do you want to pay off your loans? (if applicable)

12. What do you want? Awards/Recognition, Money, Name in Newspaper/online
    Clearly articulate what you want!

13. Next Level Goal – What is the next big thing for your business?

14. Where do you see your business in one year?

15. Where do you see your business in two years?

16. Where do you see your business in five years?

17. DREAM. Spend five to ten minutes dreaming about what your most successful business looks like. Describe it here.

18. The magic formula to reaching your goals is _____ _____ _____.

19. Remember, nothing changes until you move. You must be in ACTION! From this chapter choose ONE THING that you will implement right away in your business. There may be several, but choose the one that excites you and makes the biggest impact on your business.

20. Now go back and add dates for completion of your ONE THING. Put it on your calendar right now!

_____

Staying on track is easier when you have some support. Join your tribe on the Sharon Galluzzo Facebook page. Follow here: www.facebook.com/sharonagalluzzo

Chapter 4

Pages 33-47 in *Legendary Business: From Rats to Riche$*

Darnell Ratt

To the world at large, Darnell is an invisible rat. He has a fabulous product and all the trappings of a successful business, but no one knows about him. No one has heard of his ground-breaking invention, so no one can buy it!

1. How do the traits of Darnell Ratt manifest themselves in your business? How are you like Darnell?

2. List areas where Darnell is stealing your sustenance and making your business more difficult.

3. How many exposures to a fact or business does it take the average adult to remember it?

ADVERTISING

4. Where do you currently advertise?

5. How much does each advertising outlet cost? Add this information to the list in number 4.

6. What is your return on investment (ROI) on each outlet? Add it to the list in number 4.

7. How much do you spend per month on advertising?

8. Is this amount sufficient to get the word out about your business? If not, how much more will it take?

MARKETING

The following marketing avenues require you to research what is available in your business and physical areas. If it is online, physical boundaries do not apply. Space is supplied to write down all the information you can find. Now, go! Research, ask questions, take notes, find your answers and get the word out!

9. In-person Networking Groups

10. Online Networking Groups

11. Chambers of Commerce

12. Civic Groups

13. Press Releases -Do an internet search on how to write a press release. Hubspot's blog has a great template you can reference. Additionally, search where you can post your press release. Record your results.

14. Social Media – Research social media platforms to find where your customers hang out. List those sites here and prioritize them.

15. Referral Partners – List all the areas in your business where you think a referral partnership might be viable. (If you are a real estate agent look for house & carpet cleaners, or mortgage brokers or landscapers.) Putting this list together now will keep it top of mind when you meet others.

16. Expos and Trade Shows – Evaluate if the exposure and reach are worth both the participation fee and the time you will spend there. (What are you not doing while you are at the table? How much will you have to sell to cover the cost of the event?) Also consider the reach of the event. How many people attend? Are the attendees your customers?

17. Testimonials – Develop a system if you don't have one already. Describe it here.

18. Set a goal of how many testimonials you want each month. Write it down!

19. Workshops – A great way to gain exposure is to offer to share your knowledge with the community and or specific interest groups. Libraries and groups are always looking for speakers to fill their program calendars. Find topics that are meaningful to the audience and you could have a whole new group of folks to add to your sphere of influence. You may not be able to sell directly, but you can create an understanding of what you do and how you help that never occurred to the audience. Make sure you are giving VALUE to the audience.

20. Remember, nothing changes until you move. You must be in ACTION! From this chapter choose ONE THING that you will implement right away in your business. There may be several, but choose the one that excites you and makes the biggest impact on your business.

21. Now go back and add dates for completion of your ONE THING. Put it on your calendar right now!

   _____

As a support to *Legendary Business*, check out the "Sharon Shares" section on the www.SharonGalluzzo.com page. On this webpage are blog posts about relevant subjects pertinent to building your business and taking it to Legendary Status. Make sure you subscribe so you don't miss a thing!

Chapter 5

Pages 49-58 in *Legendary Business: From Rats to Riche$*

Charles Ratt

Charles has really good reasons for really bad customer service. His attitude and customer approach costs him business. He doesn't understand or appreciate the advantage satisfied and happy customers provide to business success.

1. How do the traits of Charles Ratt manifest themselves in your business? How are you like Charles?

2. List areas where Charles is stealing your sustenance and making your business more difficult.

3. How can eliminating these traits make your business more Legendary?

4. Many areas for improvement were listed in the book. What ideas, problems or challenges came to YOUR mind while reading that were not included in the book?

5. Of the things you listed in question 4, which are pertinent to your business? If they are problem areas (rats!) for you, add them to the list you made in questions number 2.

6. What types of customer behaviors bring out the Charles Ratt in you?

7. What personal frustrations cause you to let Charles Ratt come out? (for example: interruptions, repetitive tasks, etc.)

8. How can you develop the art of customer service with your clients? Be specific!

9. How can you take the idea of, "Here to help you," and translate it into customer service gold in your business? Sketch out a plan here that you will implement later. (Don't forget to come back and do it!)

10. Why do customers do business with you? (Hint: this IS a trick question)

11. Describe a time you let your mood or circumstances cause you to give bad customer service. How did the customer react? What did you learn?

12. Create a personal trigger; the "trick" you can use to bring yourself back to a place of service.

13. The most powerful marketing or advertising strategy in the word is word-of-mouth. In Chapter 4 you described your testimonial process. Here, describe how and where you can use the testimonials to make the greatest effect and reach for your business. Be specific about where customers can read all about you and your amazing business.

14. What are a few steps you can take if a customer puts a bad review about your business online?

15. Remember, nothing changes until you move. You must be in ACTION! From this chapter choose ONE THING that you will implement right away in your business. There may be several, but choose the one that excites you and makes the biggest impact on your business.

16. Now go back and add dates for completion of your ONE THING. Put it on your calendar right now!

There is lots of information on building a stronger business on the www.SharonGalluzzo.com page. Check out the "Resources" tab. Have you watched the video "Catching Kayla," yet? What are you waiting for?!?

Chapter 6

Pages 61-70 in *Legendary Business: From Rats to Riche$*

Charlotte Ratt

Charlotte TRIES everything. She is quick to jump in but doesn't have the stamina to get to the payoff before becoming distracted with something else. She spreads herself thin by doing everything without analyzing if it is right for her business.

1. How do the traits of Charlotte Ratt manifest themselves in your business? How are you like Charlotte?

2. List areas where Charlotte is stealing your sustenance and making your business more difficult.

3. How can eliminating Charlotte Ratt make your business more Legendary?

4. What types of things have you "tried" in your business and abandoned before you experienced a return on investment?

5. How can you use P.F.C. in your business to make it more legendary?

6. When an opportunity presents itself, the following questions can help you determine if you should take it. (Fill in the blanks)

    A. How will this _____ my business?

    B. Does this activity/program/opportunity get me _____ _____ _____ _____ or does it just absorb my time?

    C. Are my customers in this _____?

7. Of all the social media platforms out there, which actually work for your business? Which platforms are your customers using? Which provide the most effective use of time?

8. Are there any tasks, projects or initiatives that you have started and not completed that you believe will really help your business? List them here.

9. Set a time limit for completion of the items you just listed in number 8. If not an actual date, a number of weeks or months for each. Then keep track of this so you can close the loop.

In Chapter 3 you listed goals for your business. Take a couple overreaching goals (goals for your whole business) and answer questions 10-12.

10. What do you want to achieve this month, quarter and year?

11. What activities can you complete that get you closer to those goals?

12. Schedule times to follow up on these activities so that you do them consistently.

13. Why do you do what you do? Why are you in this business?

Understanding where your business goals and activities fall on the Five Levels of Commitment is very powerful. Here they are again:

1- Don't Care
2- Wishing, Hoping, Praying
3- Trying
4- Committed Unless
5- Committed Whatever It Takes

14. What areas of your business fall under Level 1-Don't Care? Brainstorm here some ideas to implement that will move them to Level 2 or higher.

15. What areas of your business fall under Level 2-Wishing, Hoping, Praying? Brainstorm here some ideas to implement that will move them to Level 3 or higher.

16. What areas of your business fall under Level 3-Trying? Brainstorm here some ideas to implement that will move them to Level 4 or higher.

17. What areas of your business fall under Level 4-Committed Unless?

18. What kinds of things comprise the "UNLESS" in the answers to question 17? Do these excuses negatively effect your business?

19. Many areas for improvement were listed in the book. What ideas, problems, challenges came to YOUR mind that we not listed in the book.

20. Remember, nothing changes until you move. You must be in ACTION! From this chapter choose ONE THING that you will implement right away in your business. There may be several, but choose the one that excites you and makes the biggest impact on your business.

21. Now go back and add dates for completion of your ONE THING. Put it on your calendar right now!

It takes a village to build a business. Have you joined The PLAN Piper Village on Facebook? This private group just for you to get advice, tips, answers to trick questions and lots more! Ask to join here: https://www.facebook.com/groups/ThePLANPiper/

Chapter 7

Pages 73-78 in *Legendary Business: From Rats to Riche$*

ACTION TEAM

Hamelin got help, and so should you!

When you are in business for yourself, YOU have to be the motivator! No one is going to come into your business and do the work for you. However, just because you are in business for yourself, doesn't mean you have to do it alone.

Surround yourself with a team of people who can help you navigate the ups and downs of business life: your ACTION TEAM. It will enable you to get closer to your goals, and keep yourself moving forward.

Brainstorm the people you would like to add to your ACTION TEAM. List their names below.

Your Opposite

True Believer

One Level Up

Different Brain

Accountability Partner

Otherwise Gifted

Your Tribe

Remember, nothing changes until you move.
You must be in ACTION!
Complete your team and
get to work on making your business legendary!

Chapter 8

Pages 81-84 in *Legendary Business: From Rats to Riche$*

Now It's Your Turn

Do not fall into the trap of all information and no follow through. Don't be Charlotte! Pick the ONE THING that you want to change first.

Take the best idea in the book. The one that makes you most excited and will help your business the most. Just one, and implement it right away. Once you have the ONE THING, brainstorm if necessary. Visualize yourself raking in the money from the ONE THING. Think better on the run? Grab your phone and record a voice memo with all the great ideas you have on ways to implement the ONE THING.

Focus on ONE THING. Do the legwork to make the idea come to life. Be committed to what needs to be done to get ready, implement and follow up.

Remember P.F.C. Planning, Follow-Through and Consistency. Make the plan to determine where you are going, implement the follow-through to make it effective and strive for consistency to move your business forward.

Once you have the ONE THING implemented, go back and do ONE THING MORE. Start again; brainstorm, visualize and implement the idea, get it going, improving your business. Continue this process until you've removed all the rats from your business.

List the ONE THING Here

See, here's the thing. I BELIEVE IN YOU! I know that you are a talented Pied Piper and you CAN lead the rats from your business and find the success of your dreams!

What's Next?

Would you like to stay connected? Do you want to be part of a business community that cares about one another? Do you believe that it takes a village to run a business?

Go to www.SharonGalluzzo.com and connect with me! On the website you'll find all my connections for social media, resources, blog posts, updates, words of encouragement and much more. I really want to know what you are doing!

> I want to hear your success stories!
> > I want to hear your questions!
> I want you to succeed beyond your wildest dreams!
> > I want to know that you defined success and you achieved it!
> So, keep in touch!

If you really enjoyed this book and workbook, please tell a friend or leave a review online. We are all better together. Pay it forward.

All the best,

Sharon

__A rising tide lifts all boats.__

CPSIA information can be obtained
at www.ICGtesting.com
Printed in the USA
BVOW03s0337100317
478288BV00004B/16/P